AUTUMN SPLENDOR
Folk Art Quilts and Projects

By DAWN HEESE

AUTUMN SPLENDOR
Folk Art Quilts and Projects

By Dawn Heese

Editor: Kimber Mitchell
Designer: Bob Deck
Photography: Aaron T. Leimkuehler
Illustration: Eric Sears
Technical Editor: Nan Powell
Photo Editor: Jo Ann Groves

Published by:
Kansas City Star Books
1729 Grand Blvd.
Kansas City, Missouri, USA 64108

Kansas City Star Quilts moves quickly to publicize corrections to our books.
You can find corrections at www.KansasCityStarQuilts.com, then click on 'Corrections.'

First edition, first printing
ISBN: 978-1-61169-137-5

Library of Congress Control Number: 2014943463

Printed in the United States of America by Walsworth Publishing Co., Marceline, MO

To order bulk copies, call StarInfo at (816) 234-4473; to order single copies, call (816) 234-4242.

KANSAS CITY STAR
QUILTS
Continuing the Tradition
KansasCityStarQuilts.com

ABOUT THE AUTHOR

Dawn Heese is a third-generation quilter and cross stitcher. Inspired by a quilt in a magazine, she bought her first rotary cutter and mat in 1999 and hasn't stopped quilting since. She particularly loves needleturn appliqué and hand quilting. Her love of traditional designs stems from fond childhood memories of being surrounded by quilts. Dawn lives in Columbia, Missouri, where she works part time as a hairstylist. Mom to two grown sons, she is also a member of the Boonslick Trail Quilters Guild as well as several sewing groups. She teaches and presents trunk shows at quilt shops and guilds nationwide. Dawn has her own pattern company, Linen Closet Designs, and her designs have been featured in national and international magazines. This is her fifth book with Kansas City Star Quilts. Follow Dawn's quilting adventures at www.dawnheesequilts.blogspot.com and www.facebook.com/LinenClosetDesigns.

TABLE *of* CONTENTS

INTRODUCTION

Autumn is my favorite of all the seasons, and October is the best the season has to offer. The days are still warm enough to be outside but the mornings are crisp. You can feel change in the air as we say goodbye to summer and look forward to the succession of holiday celebrations soon to come.

I have more decorations for fall and Halloween than for any other holiday or season. I eagerly count down the days until September arrives when I start pulling all of them out of closets and boxes to transform my home with the cozy colors and scents of the season. I have stacks of pumpkin-themed quilts, stitchery and prints.

In creating this autumn-inspired book, I wanted designs that celebrated the season, only with a different feel than the typical motifs you see in autumn quilts and projects. I couldn't help but add a couple of patterns that feature pumpkins, but for the most part, this book's quilts and projects take a different twist on the autumn theme than you might expect. So if you think you couldn't possibly need any more fall projects, think again! You haven't seen what I have in store for you!

Enjoy!

Dawn

DEDICATION

For Ann and Nancy, Tina and Angi. You know why.

ACKNOWLEDGMENTS

I want to give a big thanks to all the behind-the-scenes people who helped make this book a reality. They are the ones who really worked to bring my vision to life. Who would have thought it possible that this is my fifth book with them!

First, I must thank Doug Weaver. There would be no books without his belief in my ideas.

To Kimber Mitchell, my editor and friend, who I worked with on all five of my Kansas City Star Quilts books. She is an outstanding partner in the book editing process.

To Bob Deck, my graphic designer, who has also worked with me on all five books. Bob takes all the content, dresses it up and turns it into a real book.

To Aaron Leimkuehler, my photographer. Aaron has an eye like no other. His photography is outstanding and one of the defining factors of Kansas City Star Quilts books.

To Jo Ann Groves, who color-corrects all the photos in the book, making sure each looks their finest.

To Nan Powell, my technical editor, who checks my math and calculations so you don't find any errors!

To Eric Sears, my illustrator, who creates all the helpful diagrams and templates you see in this book so that the instructions are easy to follow.

To Janet Hollandsworth for so graciously taking on my two quilts and working her quilting magic on them at a moment's notice.

To Tammy Meador and Lori Fischer for the use of the fall foliage at the photo shoot.

And last but not least, to Valdani Threads for providing the perle cotton used in the quilts that were stitched in the Big Stitch method.

NEEDLETURN APPLIQUÉ

There are many ways to appliqué. My way is not the "right way," just the method that works best for me. I love to appliqué by hand but I don't like to spend my time doing prep work. I prefer to get right to the stitching! Because I carry my appliqué with me practically everywhere I go, my method requires very few supplies so I don't have to tote a ton of them along. Here are some needleturn appliqué basics:

1. Trace the template shapes on the dull side of a piece of freezer paper. Do not add a seam allowance to the templates. Cut out the templates on the drawn line. The freezer paper will adhere to the fabric many times. If you need four of the same leaf, for example, you need only cut one paper template and reuse it.

2. When I cut my background fabric squares to size, I seal their edges with Fray Check to prevent raveling and distortion. This prevents me from having to cut the block then resize it after stitching it.

3. Fold your background fabric square in half vertically and horizontally, finger-pressing the folds. Then fold on both diagonals and finger-press. These fold lines will serve as a guide for placing the appliqué shapes on the background fabric.

4. Iron the paper templates, shiny side down, to the right side of the appliqué fabric. Using a chalk pencil (I prefer Generals brand as they mark easily), trace around the template. Make sure the line is clearly visible as this will be your turn line. Add a ⅛" – ¼" seam allowance around the template, then cut it out.

5. Pin or baste the appliqué shape in place on the background fabric square. (I like Clover appliqué pins as they have a thick shaft that keeps them from backing out of the piece. Their oval heads are also less likely to snag your thread.)

6. Sew the appliqué shapes in the order that they are layered, starting with the bottom pieces. Use the tip of your needle or a toothpick to turn under your seam allowance.

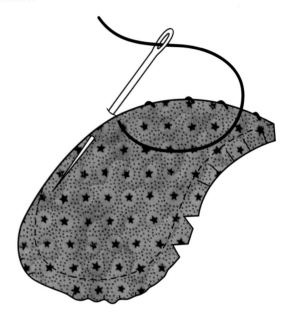

7. When appliquéing, I recommend using YLI 100-weight silk thread in a neutral color because it sinks into the fabric and practically disappears. Using a neutral color also eliminates the worry about matching all the pieces with coordinating thread colors. YLI #242 and #235 will match any color you need.

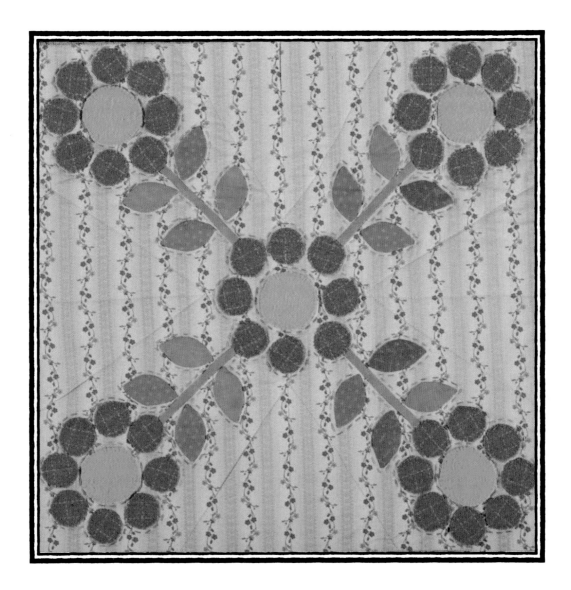

Wool Appliqué

I love the texture of wool appliqué. In addition to working with wool-on-wool, I like to mix wool with cotton backgrounds. One of the benefits of using wool is that it does not ravel, which means you do not have to turn under its edges or add a seam allowance. The process is so fast and rewarding that you will be soon be addicted to wool appliqué! Here's how to do it:

1. Trace your templates onto the dull side of a piece of freezer paper. Cut them out on the drawn line.

2. Iron the shiny side of the templates to the wool, keeping them close together. Then cut them out without a seam allowance.

3. Pin or baste the wool pieces in place on your fabric background square.

4. To stitch the wool pieces in place, I like to use wool thread that will match my appliqué piece. I prefer Aurifil Lana 12-weight thread or Simply Wool thread from The Gentle Art, Inc. To secure the appliqué pieces, take a ⅛" stitch perpendicular to the edge of the appliqué piece and about ⅛" between stitches, using a size 24 Chenille needle. This small, simple stitch will barely be noticeable as the wool thread has a texture that sinks into the wool fabric.

Velvet Appliqué

The velvet used in Early Bird on page 54 is an over-dyed cotton velvet from Blackberry Primitives. Because it is cotton, it is not slippery like traditional velvets. As a result, it is easy to work with. It does ravel, however, so you must turn under its edges. To stitch it in place, I use a size 24 chenille needle and wool thread, just as I do for wool appliqué. I needle-turn the edge, one stitch at a time, and take a little deeper stitch than usual into the appliqué piece. I don't worry about the stitch showing as the wool thread blends nicely with the velvet nap.

Stitch Guide

The following stitches are used in some of the projects in this book. When you see them listed in the instructions, come back here for guidance on how to make them if needed.

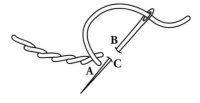

Stem Stitch

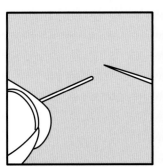 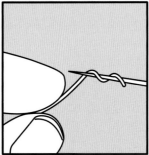 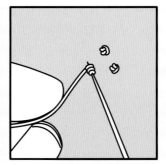 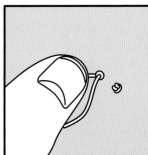

French Knot

Quilts

SPLENDOR

Hand appliquéd and machine quilted by Dawn Heese

For this design, I wanted something fall in flavor with a touch of blooms from previous seasons. You can hardly create a true folk art quilt without tulips as the two are practically synonymous. So I took some artistic license with the flowers. Even though this quilt evokes a warm autumn feel, it would make an inviting focal point in your home year round.

FABRIC REQUIREMENTS

4⅞ yards tan print for block backgrounds
   and outer border
2¼ yards assorted black prints for appliqué,
   inner border and binding
3 fat quarters red prints for appliqué
2 fat quarters orange prints for appliqué
2¼ yards total of assorted green prints for appliqué
⅓ yard total of assorted blue prints for appliqué
1 fat quarter gold print for appliqué
Green embroidery floss to match fabrics

CUTTING INSTRUCTIONS

Templates do not include a seam allowance.

From tan print, cut:
• 9—20½" squares for appliqué blocks
• 12—3" x 20½" rectangles for sashing strips
• 8—5½" strips the width of fabric for outer border

From assorted black prints, cut:
• 7—3" strips the width of fabric for inner border
• 4—3" squares for sashing

From assorted color prints listed in the Fabric Requirements, cut the appliqué shapes from templates on pages 65–72.

"The foliage has been losing its freshness through the month of August, and here and there a yellow leaf shows itself like the first gray hair amidst the locks of a beauty who has seen one season too many ... September is dressing herself in showy dahlias and splendid marigolds and starry zinnias. October, the extravagant sister, has ordered an immense amount of the most gorgeous forest tapestry for her grand reception."

~OLIVER WENDELL HOLMES

SPLENDOR

FINISHED QUILT SIZE: 80" x 80"
FINISHED BLOCK SIZE: 20" x 20"

SEWING INSTRUCTIONS

Vase Blocks

Seal the edges of 4—20½" tan print background squares with Fray Check to prevent raveling and distortion. Referring to the following photo for placement, appliqué the pieces to the prepared 20½" background square. Make stems with a ¼" bias tape maker. Using 2 strands of floss and a stem stitch, make curly vines. A French knot is made at the end of each vine by wrapping the needle 4 times. Make a total of 4 Vase blocks.

Crossing Blocks

Seal the edges of 4—20½" tan print background squares with Fray Check to prevent raveling and distortion. Referring to the following photo for placement, appliqué the pieces to the prepared 20½" background square. Make a total of 4 Crossing blocks.

Center Block

Seal the edges of 1—20½" tan print background square with Fray Check to prevent raveling and distortion. Referring to the following photo for placement, appliqué the pieces to the prepared 20½" background square. Make stems with a ¼" bias tape maker. Using 2 strands of floss and a stem stitch, make curly vines.

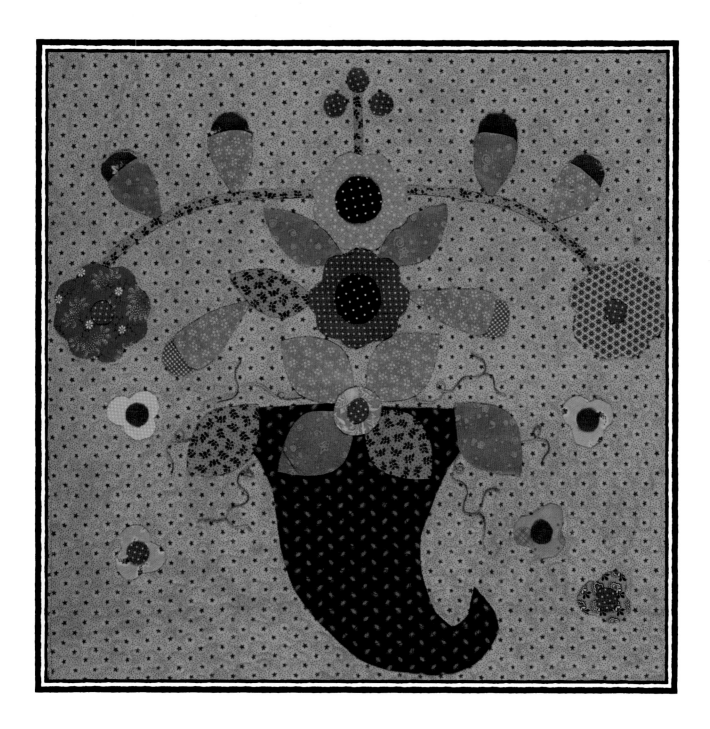

Sashing

Seal the edges of the 12—3" x 20½" tan print strips with Fray Check to prevent raveling and distortion. Referring to the following diagram, appliqué 2 black triangles to a prepared 3" x 20½" tan print strip.

Quilt Assembly

1. Referring to the following diagram, sew together 3 appliqué blocks and 2 sashing strips, carefully noting the order in which the appliqué blocks should appear. Repeat to make a total of 3 rows. (The below diagram shows the top row.)

2. Referring to the following diagram, sew together 3 sashing strips and 2—3" black print squares to create a sashing row. Repeat to make a total of 2 rows.

3. Referring to the quilt assembly diagram on page 19, join the rows from steps 1 and 2 to complete the quilt center.

4. Join the 3" x WOF black print inner border strips, then cut them to create 2—3" x 65½" strips and 2—3" x 70½" strips. Referring to the quilt assembly diagram, sew the 2—3" x 65½" strips to the sides of the quilt center. Then sew the 2—3" x 70½" strips to the top and bottom of the quilt top.

5. Join the 5½" x WOF tan print outer border strips, then cut them to create 2—5½" x 70½" strips and 2—5½" x 80½" strips. Referring to the quilt assembly diagram, sew the 2—5½" x 70½" strips to the sides of the quilt top. Then sew the 2—5½" x 80½" strips to the top and bottom of the quilt top.

6. Sandwich the quilt top, batting and backing; baste. Quilt as desired, then bind. Dawn machine quilted hers, using a stipple in the background and outer border and wavy lines in the inner border and sashing triangles.

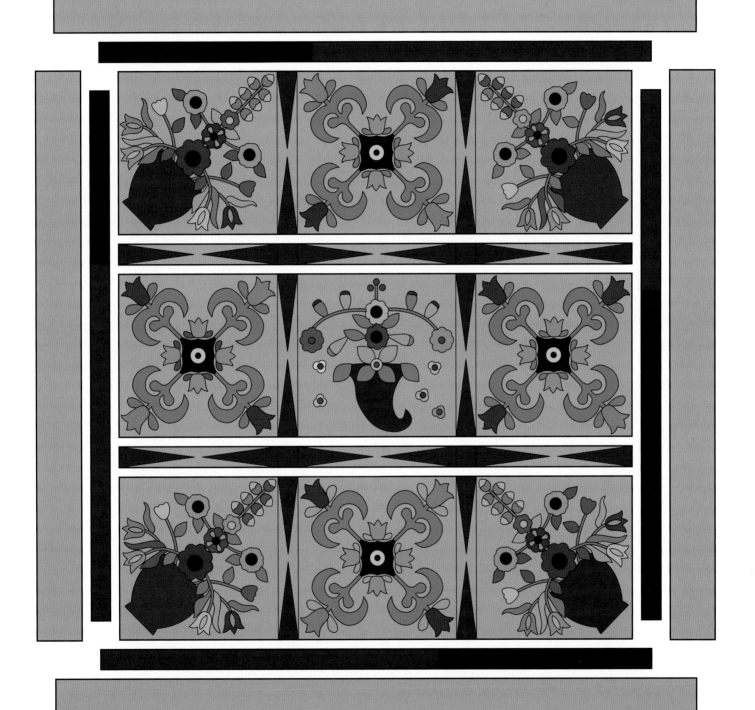

QUILT ASSEMBLY DIAGRAM

FESTIVAL

Machine pieced by Dawn Heese

Machine quilted by
Janet Hollandsworth

I love this quilt because it combines my many loves—fast-to-piece big blocks, reproduction fabrics and warm fall colors. At 21" square, the blocks are big and come together quickly. The mixture of black and orange blocks creates the perfect color palette to warm your bed throughout the season.

> *"For man, autumn is a time of harvest, of gathering together. For nature, it is a time of sowing, of scattering abroad."*
> ~EDWIN WAY TEALE,
> "AUTUMN ACROSS AMERICA"

FABRIC REQUIREMENTS

4½ yards black print for blocks, border and binding
4 yards total of assorted cream prints for blocks
2¼ yards total of assorted orange/gold prints for blocks

CUTTING INSTRUCTIONS

From assorted cream prints, cut:
• 64—5½" squares for blocks
• 128—4⅜" squares, then cut them once diagonally from corner to corner to yield a total of 256 triangles for blocks
• 32—4⅜" squares for blocks

From assorted orange/gold prints, cut:
• 32—5½" squares for blocks
• 64—4⅜" squares, then cut them once diagonally from corner to corner to yield a total of 128 triangles for blocks
• 16—4⅜" squares for blocks

From black print, cut:
• 32—5½" squares for blocks
• 64—4⅜" squares, then cut them once diagonally from corner to corner to yield a total of 128 triangles for blocks
• 16—4⅜" squares for blocks
• 10—5½" strips the width of fabric for outer border

FESTIVAL

FINISHED QUILT SIZE: 94" X 94"
FINISHED BLOCK SIZE: 21" X 21"

SEWING INSTRUCTIONS

Sew with a scant ¼" seam allowance.

Blocks

1. On the wrong side of the 4⅜" cream print squares, draw a diagonal line from corner to corner.

2. With right sides together, layer a marked cream square on top of a 4⅜" orange/gold square. Sew a ¼" seam on both sides of the drawn line, then cut on the drawn line and press open to yield 2 half-square-triangle units.

3. Repeat step 2 for the remaining 4⅜" orange/gold squares and the remaining 4⅜" black squares to yield a total of 32 orange/gold half-square-triangle units and 32 black half-square-triangle units.

4. Referring to the following diagrams for placement, sew together 4 orange/gold half-square-triangle units from the previous step to create a Pinwheel unit. Repeat with the remaining orange/gold half-square-triangle units as well as the black half-square-triangle units from the previous step to create a total of 8 orange/gold Pinwheel units and 8 black Pinwheel units.

5. Sew a black triangle to one side of a 5½" cream print square, then press back the triangle. Sew an orange/gold triangle to the opposite side of the 5½" cream print square, then press it back. Repeat for the remaining 2 sides to complete a square-in-a-square unit. Repeat this step to make a total of 64 square-in-a-square units.

6. Sew a cream triangle to one side of a 5½" black print square, then press back the triangle. Sew a cream triangle to the opposite side of the 5½" black print square, then press it back. Repeat for the remaining 2 sides to complete a square-in-a-square unit. Repeat this step to make a total of 32 square-in-a-square units.

7. Sew a cream print triangle to one side of a 5½" orange/gold print square, then press back the triangle. Sew a cream print triangle to the opposite side of the 5½" orange/gold print square, then press it back. Repeat for the remaining 2 sides to complete a square-in-a-square unit. Repeat this step to make a total of 32 square-in-a-square units.

8. Referring to the following diagram, join 4 units from step 5, 4 units from step 7, and 1 black Pinwheel unit to complete a block. Repeat to create a total of 8 blocks.

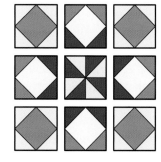 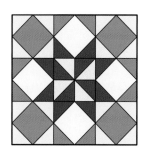

9. Referring to the following diagram, join 4 units from step 5, 4 units from step 6, and an orange/gold Pinwheel unit to complete a block. Repeat to create a total of 8 blocks.

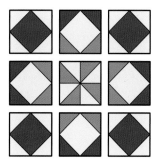 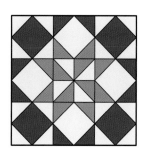

Quilt Assembly

1. Referring to the quilt assembly diagram on page 25, sew together the blocks from steps 8 and 9 in the Blocks section into 4 rows of 4 blocks each to create the quilt center.

2. Join the 5½" x WOF border strips, then cut them to create 2—5½" x 84½" strips and 2—5½" x 94½" strips. Referring to the quilt assembly diagram, sew the 2—5½" x 84½" strips to the sides of the quilt center. Then sew the 2—5½" x 94½" strips to the top and bottom of the quilt top.

3. Sandwich the quilt top, batting and backing; baste. Quilt as desired, then bind. Janet quilted an all-over white oak pattern on Dawn's quilt.

QUILT ASSEMBLY DIAGRAM

SQUASH PATCH

Hand appliquéd and hand quilted by Dawn Heese

Dig into your scrap basket to whip up this fun fall throw. Each of the little squash blocks finishes at 4" square, making them the perfect carry-along project. With only two pieces to cut, you can have a stack of these ready to go in no time. I sorted through my stash and scraps and pulled out any fall-colored print I could find to make my quilt. Once you get started making the blocks, it is hard to stop!

"Oh how we love pumpkin season. You did know this gourd-ish squash has its own season, right? Winter, Spring, Summer, Pumpkin ... We anxiously anticipate it every year."

~Trader Joe's "Fearless Flyer,"
October 2010

FABRIC REQUIREMENTS

2½ yards cream print for background
1⅛ yards total of assorted blue prints for nine-patch blocks, 1st border, outer border and binding
½ yard orange print for nine-patch blocks and 2nd border
⅛ yard green print for pumpkin stems
1⅛ yards total of assorted blue, gold, orange, green, rust and peach prints for squash appliqué blocks

CUTTING INSTRUCTIONS

Templates do not include a seam allowance.

From cream print, cut:
• 7—6⅞" squares, then cut them twice diagonally from corner to corner to yield a total of 28 setting triangles
• 89—4½" squares for appliqué blocks
• 2—3¾" squares, then cut them once diagonally from corner to corner to yield a total of 4 corner triangles
• 2—1⅞" x 37½" strips for side nine-patch blocks
• 4—1⅞" x 22½" strips for side nine-patch blocks
• 2—1⅞" x 7½" strips for corner nine-patch blocks

From blue print, cut:
• 11—1" strips the width of fabric for 1st and outer borders
• 2—1⅞" x 37½" strips for side nine-patch blocks
• 2—1⅞" x 22½" strips for side nine-patch blocks
• 2—1⅞" x 7½" strips for corner nine-patch blocks

From orange print, cut:
• 6—1¼" strips the width of fabric for 2nd border
• 2—1⅞" x 37½" strips for side nine-patch blocks
• 2—1⅞" x 7½" for corner nine-patch blocks

From assorted color prints listed in the Fabric Requirements, cut 89 squashes and stems from templates on page 76.

SQUASH PATCH

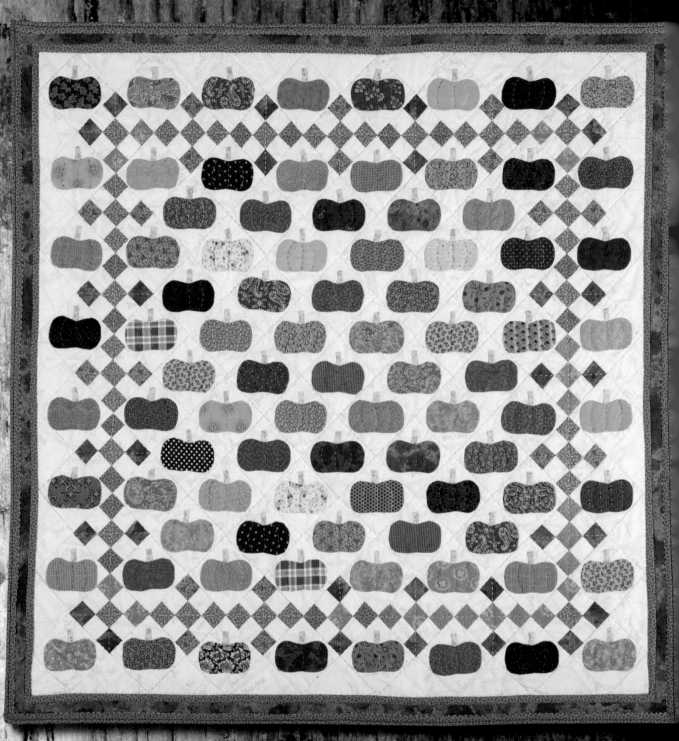

FINISHED QUILT SIZE: 48¾" x 48¾"
FINISHED BLOCK SIZE: 4" x 4"

SEWING INSTRUCTIONS

Squash Block

Seal the edges of the 89—4½" cream print squares with Fray Check to prevent raveling and distortion. Referring to the following diagram, appliqué the squashes and stems to the cream print squares.

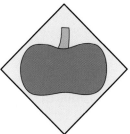

Side Nine-Patch Blocks

These are the nine-patch blocks along the sides, top and bottom of the quilt – with the exception of the 4 in the corners. The color placement within these blocks differs from that of the corner nine-patch blocks.

1. Sew a 1⅞" x 37½" blue print strip to 1 side of a 1⅞" x 37½" cream strip. Press the seam toward the blue strip. Sew an orange print strip to the opposite side of the cream strip and press the seam toward the orange print strip. Repeat to make 2 of these strip sets.

2. Cut each strip set from the previous step into 20—1⅞"-wide segments for a total of 40 segments.

3. Sew a 1⅞" x 22½" cream print strip to one side of a 1⅞" x 22½" blue strip. Press the seam toward the blue strip. Sew a second cream strip to the opposite side of the blue strip and press the seam toward the blue strip. Make 2 of these strip sets.

4. Cut each strip set from the previous step into 12—1⅞"-wide segments for a total of 24 segments. Set aside 4 of these for the corner nine-patch blocks, which you will make later.

5. Referring to the following diagram, sew together 1 segment from step 4 and 2 segments from step 2 to create a nine-patch block. Repeat to create a total of 20 nine-patch blocks.

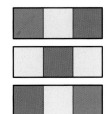

Corner Nine-Patch Blocks

1. Sew 1—1⅞" x 7½" blue print strip to 1 side of a 1⅞" x 7½" cream print strip. Press the seam toward the blue strip. Sew a second blue strip to the opposite side of the cream strip. Press the seam toward the blue strip.

2. Cut the strip set from the previous step into 4—1⅞"-wide segments.

3. Sew 1—1⅞" x 7½" orange print strip to 1 side of a 1⅞" x 7½" cream strip. Press the seam toward the orange strip. Sew a second orange strip to the opposite side of the cream strip. Press the seam toward the orange strip.

4. Cut the strip set from the previous step into 4—1⅞"-wide segments.

5. Join the segments from steps 2 and 4 with the 4 segments set aside from the side nine-patch blocks to create 4 corner nine-patch blocks.

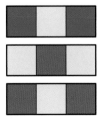

Quilt Assembly

1. Referring to the quilt assembly diagram on page 31, sew together the squash blocks, side nine-patch blocks, corner nine-patch blocks, and setting triangles into diagonal rows. Then join the rows to complete the quilt center.

2. Join the 1" x WOF 1st and outer border blue strips, then cut them to create 2—1" x 45¾" strips, 2—1" x 46¾" strips, 2—1" x 48¼" strips and 2—1" x 49¼" strips. Referring to the quilt assembly diagram, sew the 2—1" x 45¾" strips to the sides of the quilt center. Then sew the 2—1" x 46¾" strips to the top and bottom of the quilt top. Reserve the remaining ones for step 4 below.

3. Join the 1¼" x WOF 2nd border orange strips, then cut them to create 2—1¼" x 46¾" strips and 2—1¼" x 49¼" strips. Referring to the quilt assembly diagram, sew the 2—1¼" x 46¾" strips to the sides of the quilt top. Then sew the 2—1¼" x 49¼" strips to the top and bottom of the quilt top.

4. Referring to the quilt assembly diagram, sew the 2—1" x 48¼" blue outer border strips from step 2 to the sides of the quilt top. Then sew the 2—1" x 49¼" blue outer border strips from step 2 to the top and bottom of the quilt top.

5. Sandwich the quilt top, batting and backing; baste. Quilt as desired, then bind. Dawn quilted hers with Valdani No. 8 perle cotton and the Big Stitch method (a form of hand quilting done with a larger stitch and perle cotton).

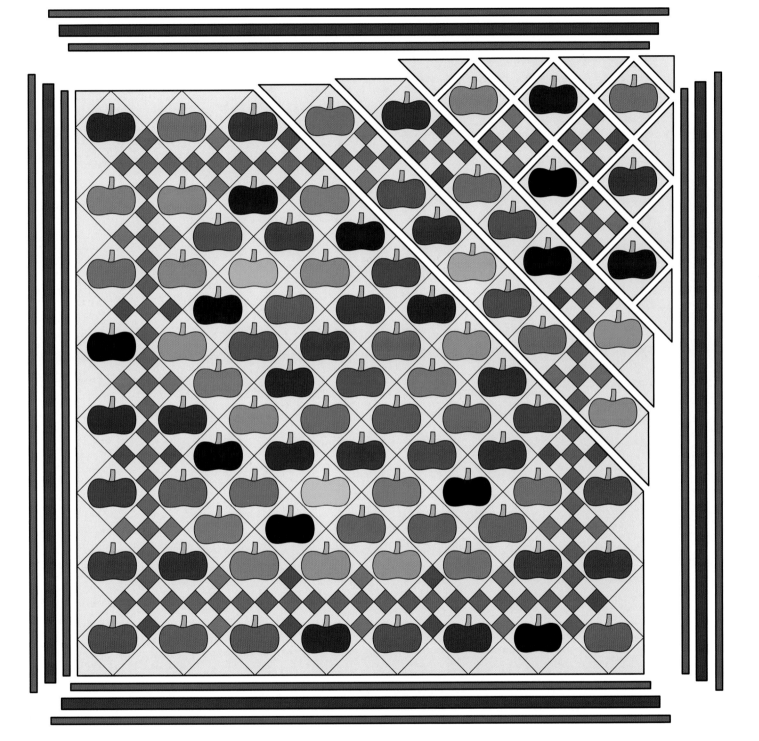

QUILT ASSEMBLY DIAGRAM

GOLDENROD

Hand appliquéd by Dawn Heese

Machine and hand quilted by Dawn Heese

Often when we think of autumn colors, we picture the rusts and oranges of fall foliage. Dusty blues are a great complement to these traditional fall colors. For a twist on tradition, I paired a dusty blue cotton background with orange and golden wool and a touch of sharp green cotton in this quilt. The wool appliqué adds texture and dimension to the simple design.

FABRIC REQUIREMENTS

2⅜ yards blue stripe for background, border, sashing and binding

1⅛ yard total of assorted green prints for appliqué and sashing

1 fat eighth gold wool for appliqué

2 fat eighths orange wool for appliqué

CUTTING INSTRUCTIONS

Templates do not include a seam allowance. Because felted wool does not fray, there is no need to turn under the edges of the appliqué pieces.

From blue stripe, cut:
- 4—18½" squares for appliqué block backgrounds
- 2—1½" x 37" strips for sashing
- 2—1½" x 41½" strips for outer border
- 3—6½" strips the width of fabric for outer border
- 5—1½" squares for nine-patch unit in sashing

From assorted green prints, cut:
- 4—1½" x 37" strips for sashing
- 2—1½" x 39½" strips for inner border
- 2—1½" x 41½" strips for inner border
- 4—1½" squares for nine-patch unit in sashing

From orange and gold wool and assorted green prints listed in the Fabric Requirements, cut flowers and leaves from appliqué templates on page 77.

GOLDENROD

FINISHED QUILT SIZE: 43" X 53"
FINISHED BLOCK SIZE: 18" X 18"

SEWING INSTRUCTIONS

Appliqué Blocks

Seal the edges of the 4—18½" blue stripe squares with Fray Check to prevent raveling and distortion. Referring to the following photo and using your favorite appliqué method, appliqué the green leaves and the gold and orange wool flowers to the prepared 18½" blue stripe square background block. Make stems with a ¼" bias tape maker. Repeat to make a total of 4 appliqué blocks.

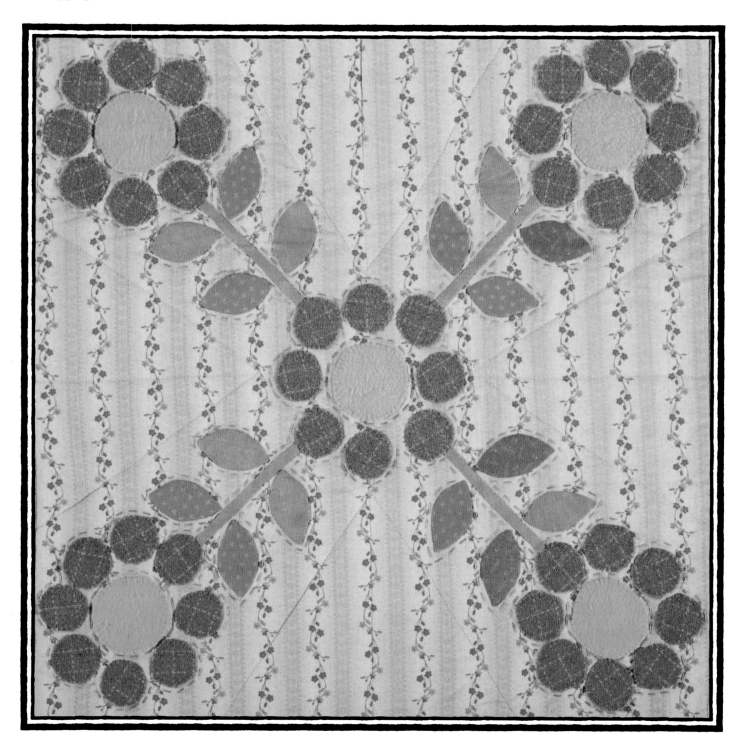

Sashing

1. Sew a 1½" x 37" green print strip to each side of a 1½" x 37" blue stripe strip. Repeat to make a total of 2 strip sets.

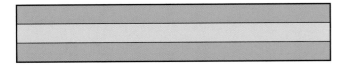

2. Cut the 2 strip sets from the previous step into 4—3½" x 18½" sashing strips.

3. Sew a 1½" blue stripe square to each side of a 1½" green print square. Repeat to make a total of 2 units.

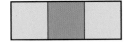

4. Sew a 1½" green print square to each side of a 1½" blue stripe square.

5. Join the units from steps 3 and 4 to create a nine-patch block.

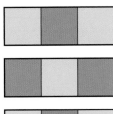
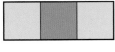

6. Sew together 2 finished appliqué blocks and a sashing strip to create a row. Repeat to make a total of 2 rows.

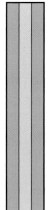

7. Sew together 2 sashing strips and the nine-patch block to create the center sashing strip.

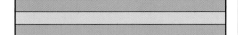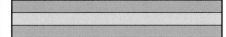

Quilt Assembly

1. Referring to the quilt assembly diagram on page 38, sew together the 2 rows from step 6 and 1 sashing strip from step 7 in the Sashing section to complete the quilt center.

2. Referring to the quilt assembly diagram, sew the 2—1½" x 39½" green inner border strips to each side of the quilt center. Then sew the 2—1½" x 41½" green inner border strips to the top and bottom of the quilt top.

3. Referring to the quilt assembly diagram, sew the 2—1½" x 41½" blue outer border strips to the sides of the quilt top.

4. Cut 1 of the 6½" x WOF blue strips in half to create 2 strips. Sew 1 to each of the remaining 2—6½" x WOF strips, then cut each to measure 6½" x 43½". Referring to the quilt assembly diagram, sew those 2 outer border strips to the top and bottom of the quilt top.

5. Sandwich the quilt top, batting and backing; baste. Quilt as desired, then bind. Dawn quilted hers with Valdani No. 8 perle cotton and the Big Stitch method (a form of hand quilting done with a larger stitch and perle cotton).

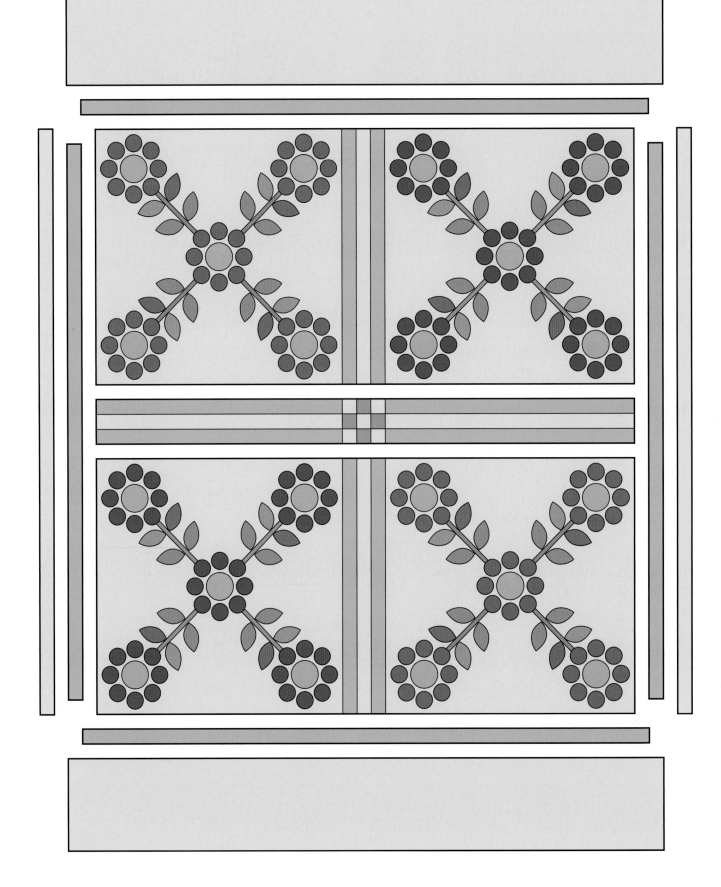

QUILT ASSEMBLY DIAGRAM

Hallow's Eve

Hand appliquéd and machine pieced by Dawn Heese

Machine quilted by Tammy Bush

"Listen! the wind is rising, and the air is wild with leaves. We have had our summer evenings, now for October eves."
~Humbert Wolfe, "P.L.M.: Peoples, Landfalls, Mountains," 1936

I couldn't do an autumn-themed book without including a project just for Halloween. I love all things about that holiday. Maybe it's because my birthday is just a few days before it! For this project, I wanted a quilt large enough for a bed but one that would be fast to make since it could only be used for such a short amount of time. This quilt combines simple piecing with easy appliqué, making it perfect for beginners or a quick quilt for more experienced quilters.

FABRIC REQUIREMENTS

1¼ yards purple print for inner border and large Churn Dash block
2½ yards tan print for block backgrounds
1¼ yards total of assorted black prints for small Churn Dash blocks and cat appliqué
2⅝ yards black marble for outer border and binding
1⅛ yards total of assorted orange prints for small Churn Dash blocks and border appliqué

CUTTING INSTRUCTIONS

Templates do not include a seam allowance.

From tan print, cut:
• 2—8⅞" squares for block backgrounds
• 4—4½" x 8½" rectangles for block backgrounds
• 1—8½" square for block backgrounds
• 42—4⅞" squares for block backgrounds
• 84—2½" x 4½" rectangles for block backgrounds
• 21—4½" squares for block backgrounds

From assorted orange prints, cut:
• 22—4⅞" squares for small Churn Dash blocks
• 44—2½" x 4½" rectangles for small Churn Dash blocks
• Border appliqué stars and moon on pages 73 and 74

From black prints, cut:
• 20—4⅞" squares for small Churn Dash blocks
• 40—2½" x 4½" rectangles for small Churn Dash blocks
• Cat on page 75

From purple print, cut:
• 2—8⅞" squares for large Churn Dash block
• 4—4½" x 8½" rectangles for large Churn Dash block
• 7—3½" strips the width of fabric for inner border

From black marble, cut:
• 8—8½" strips the width of fabric for outer border

HALLOW'S EVE

FINISHED QUILT SIZE: 82" x 82"
FINISHED SMALL CHURN DASH BLOCK SIZE: 12" x 12"
FINISHED LARGE CHURN DASH BLOCK SIZE: 24" x 24"

SEWING INSTRUCTIONS

Small Churn Dash Blocks

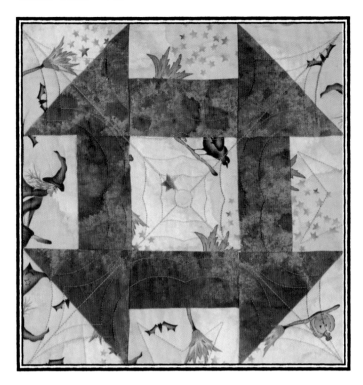

1. On the wrong side of the 42—4⅞" tan print squares, draw a diagonal line from corner to corner.

2. With right sides together, layer a marked 4⅞" tan print square on top of a 4⅞" orange square. Sew a ¼" seam on both sides of the drawn line, then cut apart on the drawn line, and press open to yield a total of 2 half-square-triangle units. Using 22 of the 4⅞" tan print squares, repeat to make a total of 44 half-square-triangle units.

3. Sew together a 2½" x 4½" tan print rectangle and 2½" x 4½" orange rectangle to create the following unit. Using 22 of the 2½" x 4½" tan print rectangles, repeat to make a total of 44 units.

4. Referring to the following diagram, sew together 4 half-square-triangle units from step 2, 4 units from step 3 and 1—4½" tan print square to create a block. Repeat to make a total of 11 tan/orange small Churn Dash blocks.

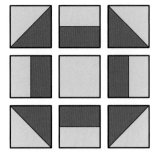

5. With right sides together, layer the remaining marked tan print squares with the 20—4⅞" black squares. Sew a ¼" seam on both sides of the drawn line, then cut apart on the drawn line, and press open to yield a total of 40 half-square-triangle units.

6. Sew together the 2½" x 4½" black rectangles with the remaining 2½" x 4½" tan rectangles to create units that look like the following one.

7. Referring to the following diagram, sew together 4 half-square-triangle units from step 5, 4 units from step 6 and 1—4½" tan print square to create a block. Repeat to make a total of 10 tan/black small Churn Dash blocks.

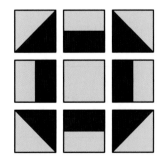

Large Churn Dash Block

1. Seal the edges of the 8½" tan print square with Fray Check to prevent raveling and distortion. Referring to the project photo on page 41 for placement, appliqué the cat shape to the prepared background print square, then set it aside.

2. On the wrong side of the 8⅞" tan print squares, draw a diagonal line from corner to corner.

3. With right sides together, layer a marked tan print square on top of an 8⅞" purple print square. Sew a ¼" seam on both sides of the drawn line, then cut apart on the drawn line, and press open to yield a total of two half-square-triangle units. Repeat this step to make a total of 4 half-square-triangle units.

4. Sew a 4½" x 8½" tan print rectangle to a 4½" x 8½" purple print rectangle to create the following unit. Repeat to make a total of 4 units.

5. Referring to following diagram, sew together the 4 half-square-triangle units from step 3, 4 units from step 4 and the 8½" appliquéd cat square to create the large Churn Dash block.

Quilt Assembly

1. Referring to the quilt assembly diagram on page 45, sew the small Churn Dash blocks and the large Churn Dash block into rows, then join the rows to create the quilt center.

2. Sew the 3½"-wide inner border purple strips end to end to create 2—3½" x 60½" strips. Then sew those 2 strips to the sides of the quilt center.

3. Sew the 3½"-wide inner border purple strips end to end to create 2—3½" x 66½" strips. Then sew those 2 strips to the top and bottom of the quilt top.

4. Sew the 8½"-wide outer border black strips end to end to create 2—8½" x 66½" strips. Then sew those 2 strips to the sides of the quilt top.

5. Sew the 8½"-wide outer border black strips end to end to create 2—8½" x 82½" strips. Then sew those 2 strips to the top and bottom of the quilt top.

6. Using your favorite appliqué method and referring to the project photo on page 41 for placement, stitch the moon and stars from the templates on page 73 and 74 to the left and bottom borders. (You do not have to follow the exact placement of Dawn's quilt. Feel free to sprinkle your stars to suit your fancy.)

7. Sandwich the quilt top, batting and backing; baste. Quilt as desired, then bind. Tammy quilted a spider web design in each of the pieced blocks and a Baptist fan design in the borders of Dawn's quilt.

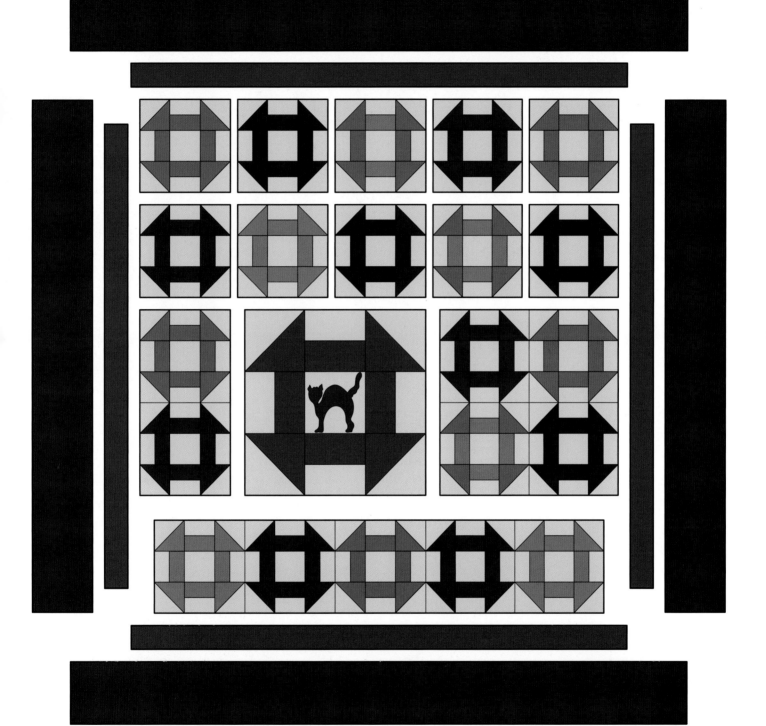

QUILT ASSEMBLY DIAGRAM

PATHWAYS

Hand appliquéd and machine pieced by Dawn Heese

Machine quilted by Janet Hollandsworth

"falling leaves
hide the path
so quietly"

~JOHN BAILEY,
"AUTUMN," FROM
"A HAIKU YEAR," 2001

One of my favorite autumn traditions is taking walks. Leaves crinkle underneath your feet, the air is crisp and invigorating and Mother Nature's colors are spectacular. I wanted to capture that feeling in this quilt. Its batik background reminds me of a sidewalk after the rain, and I have scattered leaves along it. Although it might look complicated, the Garden Maze pattern is actually simple to make with quick-piecing techniques.

FABRIC REQUIREMENTS

3 yards stone-colored batik for block backgrounds and top border
3⅛ yards total of assorted golden brown prints for blocks and appliqué
2⅛ yards total of assorted blue prints for blocks, binding and appliqué
½ yard blue-brown print for vine and stems

CUTTING INSTRUCTIONS

Templates do not include a seam allowance.

From stone-colored batik, cut:
• 2—12½" strips the width of fabric for top border
• 60—3½" x 6½" strips for blocks
• 61—4¼" squares for blocks
• 100—2" squares for blocks

From assorted golden brown prints, cut:
• 120—2" x 6½" strips for blocks
• 72—2⅝" x 9½" strips for blocks

From assorted blue prints, cut:
• 25—3½" squares for blocks
• 100—2⅜" squares for blocks

From assorted color prints listed in the Fabric Requirements, cut the leaves and berries in the top border from templates on page 76.

PATHWAYS

FINISHED QUILT SIZE: 66" x 78"
FINISHED BLOCK SIZE: 6" x 6"

SEWING INSTRUCTIONS

Rail Fence Blocks

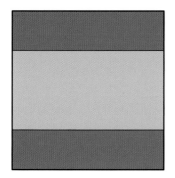

Sew a 2" x 6½" golden brown print strip to each side of a 3½" x 6½" stone-colored batik strip to make a Rail Fence block. Press the seams toward the golden brown print strips. Repeat to make a total of 60 Rail Fence blocks.

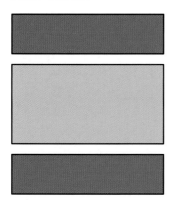

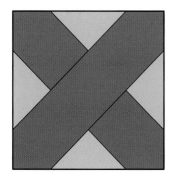

Cross Blocks

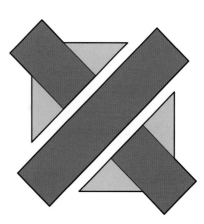

1. Cut 36 of the 4¼" stone-colored batik squares in half diagonally once from corner to corner to yield a total of 72 triangles. Fold the triangles in half and finger-press them to mark the center line of each.

2. Sew a triangle from step 1 to each side of a 2⅝" x 9½" brown print strip, aligning the centers of each. To help your block lay flat when joining the next section, press

the seams toward the stone-colored batik. Do NOT trim anything at this point. Repeat to make a total of 36 units.

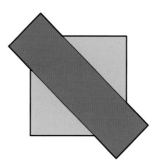

3. Cut the 36 units from the previous step in half.

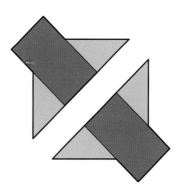

4. Sew 2 of the triangle units from the previous step to each side of a 2" x 9½" brown print strip. Repeat to make a total of 36 Cross blocks. Using a 6½" square ruler, trim the blocks to measure 6½" square.

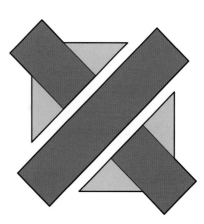

Sawtooth Star Blocks

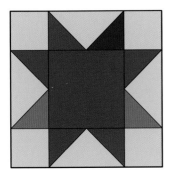

1. With right sides together, layer 2—2⅜" blue print squares on top of a 4¼" stone-colored batik square, then pin them in place. Mark a line diagonally from the top left corner to the bottom right corner through the center of the blue print squares. Then sew an accurate ¼" seam on both sides of the drawn line.

2. Cut apart the unit from the previous step on the drawn line, then press the seams toward the blue print.

3. Draw a diagonal line on the wrong side of another 2⅜" blue print square. With right sides together, layer the marked blue print square on top of a unit from the previous step. Sew a ¼" seam from both sides of the drawn line. Repeat with the remaining unit and a 2⅜" blue print square. Cut apart on the drawn lines.

4. Press open the four Flying Geese units, which will form the points of the star.

5. Repeat steps 1–4 to make 25 sets of 4 Flying Geese units.

6. Referring to the following diagram, sew together 4 Flying Geese units, 4—2" stone-colored batik squares and 1—3½" blue print square to create a Sawtooth Star block. Repeat to create a total of 25 Sawtooth Star blocks.

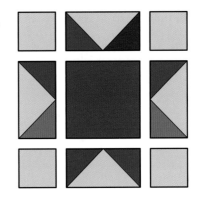

Appliqué Border

1. Sew together the 2—12½" x WOF stone-colored batik strips, then cut them to create a 12½" x 66½" strip and seal the edges with Fray Check to prevent raveling and distortion.

2. Make the large vine with a ½" bias tape maker and small stems with a ¼" bias tape maker. Referring to the project photo on page 48 for placement, appliqué the leaves, berries and vines to the stone-colored batik strip.

Quilt Assembly

1. Referring to the quilt assembly diagram on page 51, sew together 6 Cross blocks and 5 Rail Fence blocks to create a row. Repeat to create a total of 6 rows.

2. Referring to the quilt assembly diagram, sew together 6 Rail Fence blocks and 5 Sawtooth Star blocks to create a row. Repeat to create a total of 5 rows.

3. Referring to the quilt assembly diagram, join the rows from steps 1 and 2.

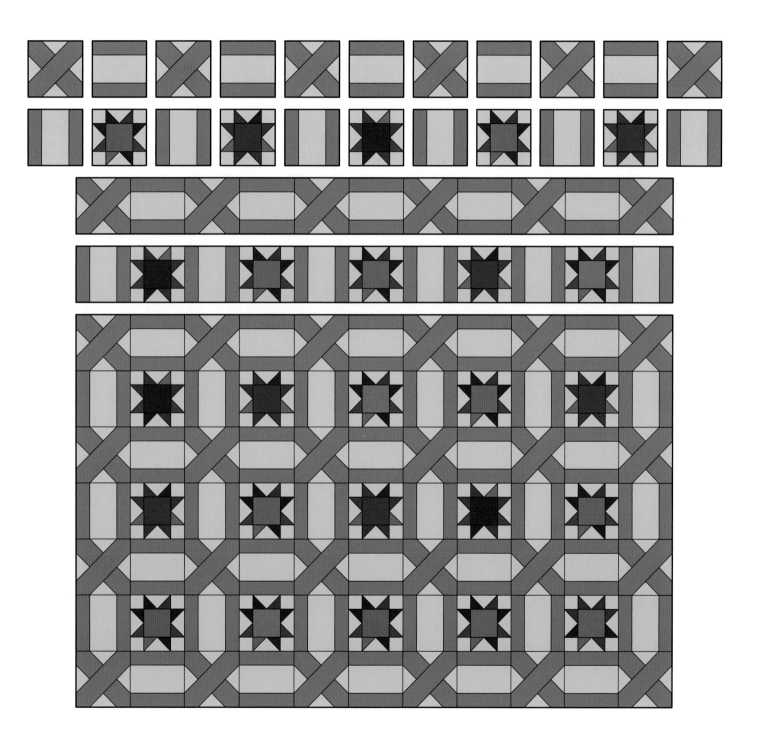

QUILT ASSEMBLY DIAGRAM

4. Referring to the following diagram, sew the finished appliquéd border to the top of the quilt top from step 3.

5. Sandwich the quilt top, batting and backing; baste. Quilt as desired, then bind. Janet created a quilting design from Dawn's appliqué design and quilted it over the pieced portion of the quilt. The border was quilted with waving lines around the appliqué.

PROJECTS

EARLY BIRD

Hand appliquéd by Dawn Heese

I recently started designing a line of dresser scarf patterns and wanted to include one in this book. Combining wool and velvet appliqué with a touch of embroidery, this little project assembles quickly and is an easy way to change out your décor. Plus, it makes a great gift. A ruffled edge adds a final flourish.

"O' pumpkin pie, your time has come 'round again and I am autumnrifically happy!"
~TERRI GUILLEMETS

FABRIC REQUIREMENTS

1 fat quarter ticking stripe for background and backing
1 fat quarter purple print for ruffle
5½" x 8" gold wool for pumpkins
3" x 6½" green wool for pumpkin stems
2" x 3½" purple wool for bird wing
3" x 7" black velvet for bird body
Green wool thread in color to match wool for stitching curly vines
Cream wool thread for French knots
Wool thread in colors that match velvet and wool appliqués
#24 Chenille needle

CUTTING INSTRUCTIONS

Templates do not include a seam allowance.

From tan ticking stripe, cut:
• 2—6½" x 21" rectangles for appliqué background and dresser scarf backing

From purple print, cut:
• 4—1½" strips the length of fat quarter for ruffle

From assorted color wools and velvet listed in Fabric Requirements, cut bird and pumpkins from templates on page 78. Be sure to add a seam allowance to the velvet bird body because velvet ravels. Wool does not ravel, so the wool pieces do not need a seam allowance.

EARLY BIRD

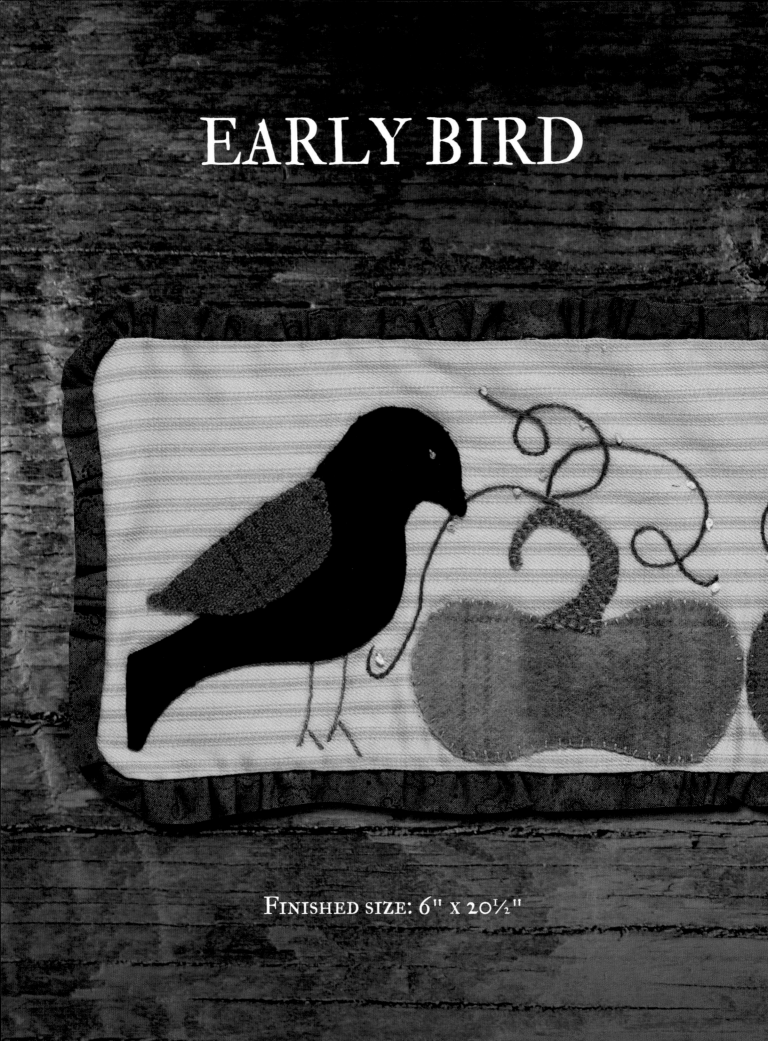

FINISHED SIZE: 6" X 20½"

SEWING INSTRUCTIONS

Appliqué

1. Seal the edges of 1 of the 6½" x 21" ticking stripe pieces with Fray Check to prevent raveling and distortion.

2. Referring to the project photo on pages 56 and 57, lay out the pumpkins, pumpkin stems, bird body and bird wing on the prepared 6½" x 21" ticking stripe piece. Using a size 24 chenille needle and 12-weight wool thread in a color that matches the appliqué, appliqué the pieces in place. (The velvet piece will need to be needle-turned because it ravels; The wool pieces, which are appliquéd with a small whipstitch, do not need to be needle-turned because they do not ravel.)

Embroidery

1. Referring to the project photo for placement, draw the vines on the appliquéd 6½" x 21" ticking stripe piece. Because this is a folk art-style project, the vines do not have to be exact. Just free-hand them.

2. Using green wool thread, stem-stitch the vines. Using the cream wool thread, make French knots by wrapping the needle three times and placing them where the cream dots are on the placement guide, below.

Ruffle

1. Join the 1½"-wide purple strips, then cut them to measure 1½" x 72". Fold the strip in half lengthwise and press as though you were making binding. Fold each end back ⅛" twice, then press. Stitch in place to make a hem on each end of the long strip.

2. Using heavy thread or perle cotton, sew a large basting stitch along the unfinished edge of the strip and pull to gather.

3. Align the raw edge of the gathered strip with the raw edges of the appliquéd piece. Adjust the gathered strip to fit, then pin it in place on the right side of the piece. Using a ⅛" seam, machine-baste the gathered strip in place.

4. With right sides together, layer the backing onto the appliquéd piece that has the ruffle basted to it. Pin the layers securely, then sew them together with a ¼" seam, leaving an opening for turning them right side out in the next step.

5. Turn the piece right side out and whipstitch the opening closed.

Harvest Fruits

Hand appliquéd and machine quilted by Dawn Heese

I love working with wool and am always looking for new and fun projects that use it. When designing this project, I wanted a wall hanging that would complement my fall décor yet be suitable for other times of the year as well. This fun design is fast to assemble, making it a great weekend project.

FABRIC REQUIREMENTS

1⅓ yards gold cotton print for quilted base (this looks like a border but the appliquéd piece is actually stitched to the top of it) and binding
16" x 22" cream wool for appliqué background
Fat quarter green wool for appliqué
6" x 7" gold wool for appliqué
3" x 7" dark blue wool for appliqué
3" x 5" medium blue wool for appliqué
6" x 7" plum wool for appliqué
5" x 5½" black wool for appliqué
24" x 30" batting
Gold No. 8 perle cotton

CUTTING INSTRUCTIONS

Templates do not include a seam allowance. Because felted wool does not fray, there is no need to turn under the edges of the appliqué pieces. For best use of fabric, it is important to cut out the items from the list below in the order in which they appear.

From gold print, trim the selvedge, then cut:
• 3—2¼" x 45" strips parallel with selvedge edge for binding
• 2—22½" x 28½" rectangles for background and backing

From cream wool, cut:
• 1—16" x 22" rectangle for appliqué background
(this does not need to be exact but should be trimmed up evenly)

From assorted color wools listed in the Fabric Requirements, cut the appliqué pieces from templates on page 77.

From green wool, cut:
All stems are non-bias
• 1—½" x 14" strip for main center stem
• 2—½" x 5¼" strips for lower stems
• 2—½" x 6¼" strips for middle stems
• 2—½" x 4¼" strips for upper stems
• 8—¼" x 2¼" strips for small stems

*"O autumn, laden with fruit, and stain'd
With the blood of the grape, pass not, but sit
Beneath my shady roof, there thou mayst rest,
And tune thy jolly voice to my fresh pipe,
And all the daughters of the year shall dance!
Sing now the lusty song of fruits and flowers."*
~William Blake, "To Autumn"

HARVEST FRUITS

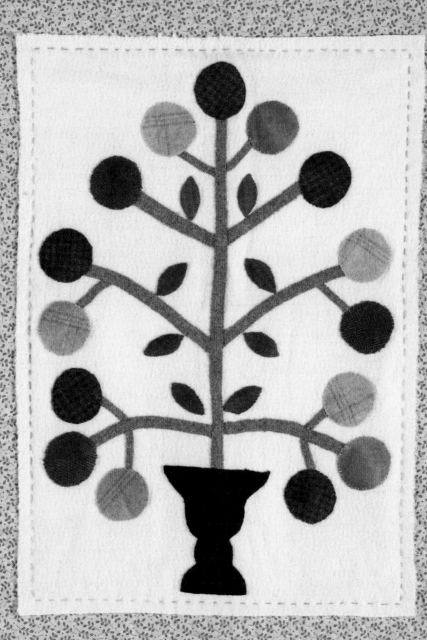

FINISHED QUILT SIZE: 22" x 28"

SEWING INSTRUCTIONS

Quilted Base

1. Make a quilt sandwich with the 2—22½" x 28½" gold print cotton pieces and the batting, then pin them securely with basting pins to prevent shifting. Quilt the piece. (It does not need to be fancy. You simply need a quilted piece to attach the appliquéd 16" x 22" cream wool background to later.) You can use your walking foot to quilt lines or a grid, or try free-motion-quilting a random pattern or stippling. Dawn stipple quilted hers as she finds that a quick and manageable way to quilt a small quilt.

2. Trim away excess batting and square up the quilt sandwich, then bind it with the 2¼"-wide gold print strips.

Appliqué

1. Referring to the diagram at left for placement, appliqué the shapes to the cream wool background.

2. With right side up, center the finished appliquéd cream wool piece from step 1 onto the gold print quilted base, then pin it in place to prevent shifting while attaching it in the next step.

3. Using the No. 8 perle cotton, stitch the appliquéd piece on top of the gold print quilted base with a primitive running stitch ½" from the edge of the wool.

Templates

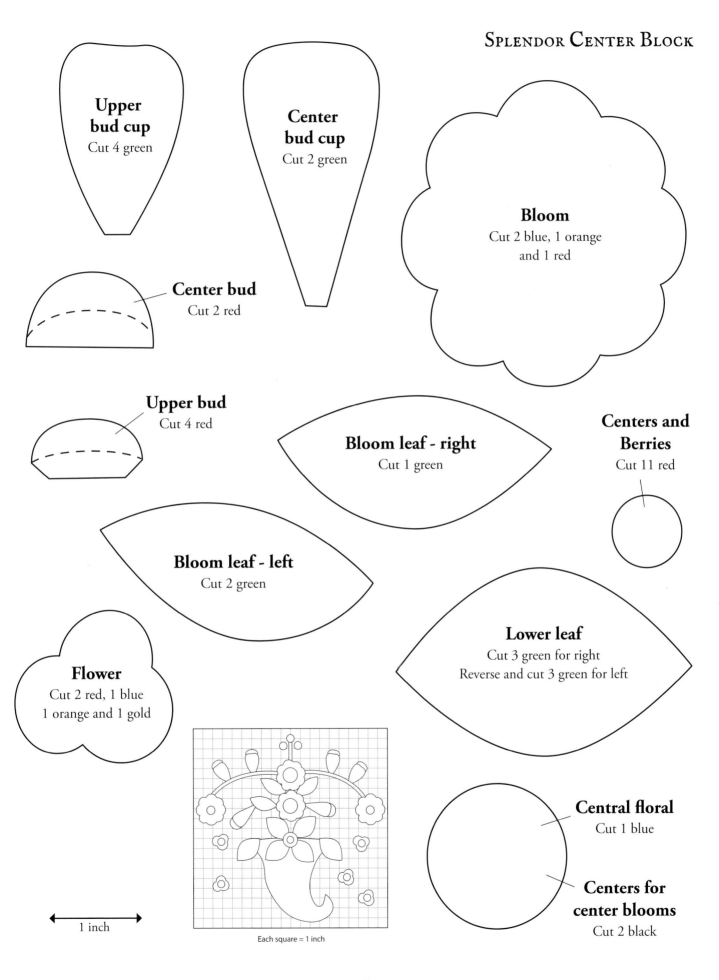

**Upper
bud cup**
Cut 4 green

**Center
bud cup**
Cut 2 green

Bloom
Cut 2 blue, 1 orange
and 1 red

Center bud
Cut 2 red

Upper bud
Cut 4 red

Bloom leaf - right
Cut 1 green

**Centers and
Berries**
Cut 11 red

Bloom leaf - left
Cut 2 green

Lower leaf
Cut 3 green for right
Reverse and cut 3 green for left

Flower
Cut 2 red, 1 blue
1 orange and 1 gold

1 inch

Each square = 1 inch

Central floral
Cut 1 blue

**Centers for
center blooms**
Cut 2 black

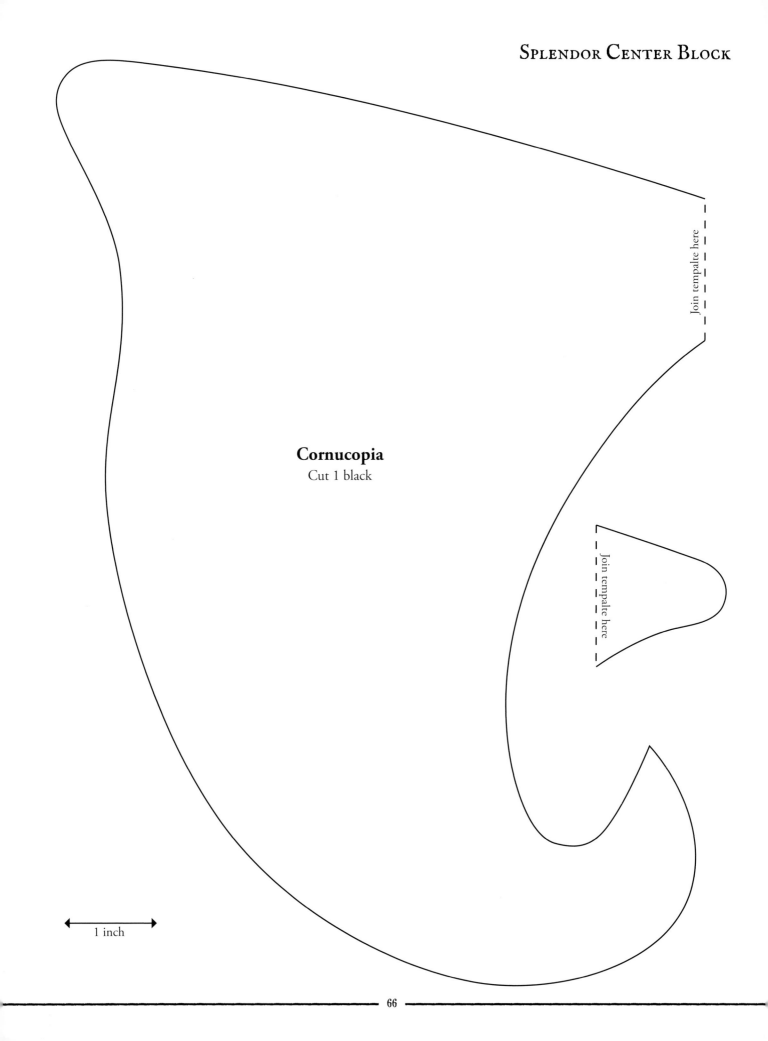

Join tempalte here

Join tempalte here

Cornucopia
Cut 1 black

1 inch

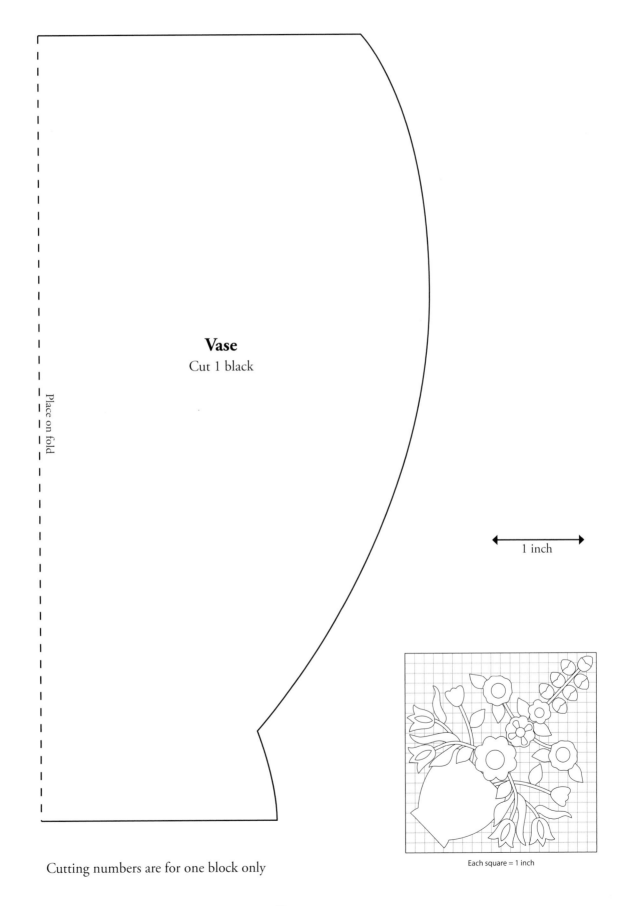

Vase

Cut 1 black

Place on fold

1 inch

Each square = 1 inch

Cutting numbers are for one block only

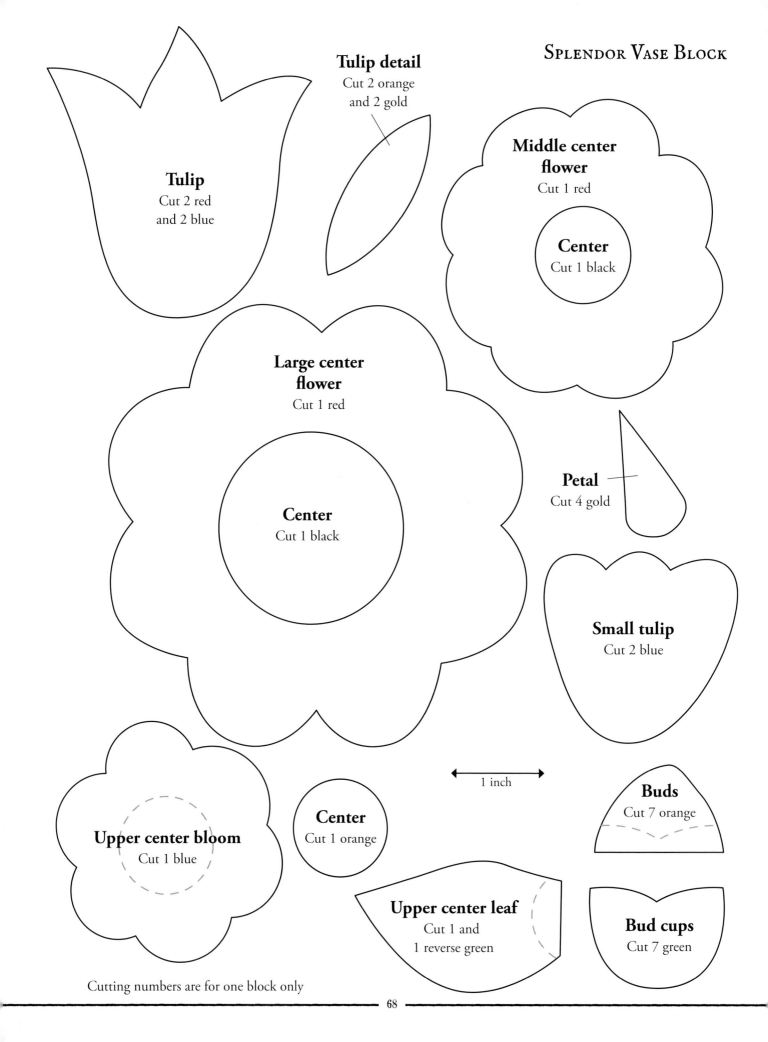

Tulip detail
Cut 2 orange
and 2 gold

Tulip
Cut 2 red
and 2 blue

**Middle center
flower**
Cut 1 red

Center
Cut 1 black

**Large center
flower**
Cut 1 red

Center
Cut 1 black

Petal
Cut 4 gold

Small tulip
Cut 2 blue

1 inch

Buds
Cut 7 orange

Upper center bloom
Cut 1 blue

Center
Cut 1 orange

Upper center leaf
Cut 1 and
1 reverse green

Bud cups
Cut 7 green

Cutting numbers are for one block only

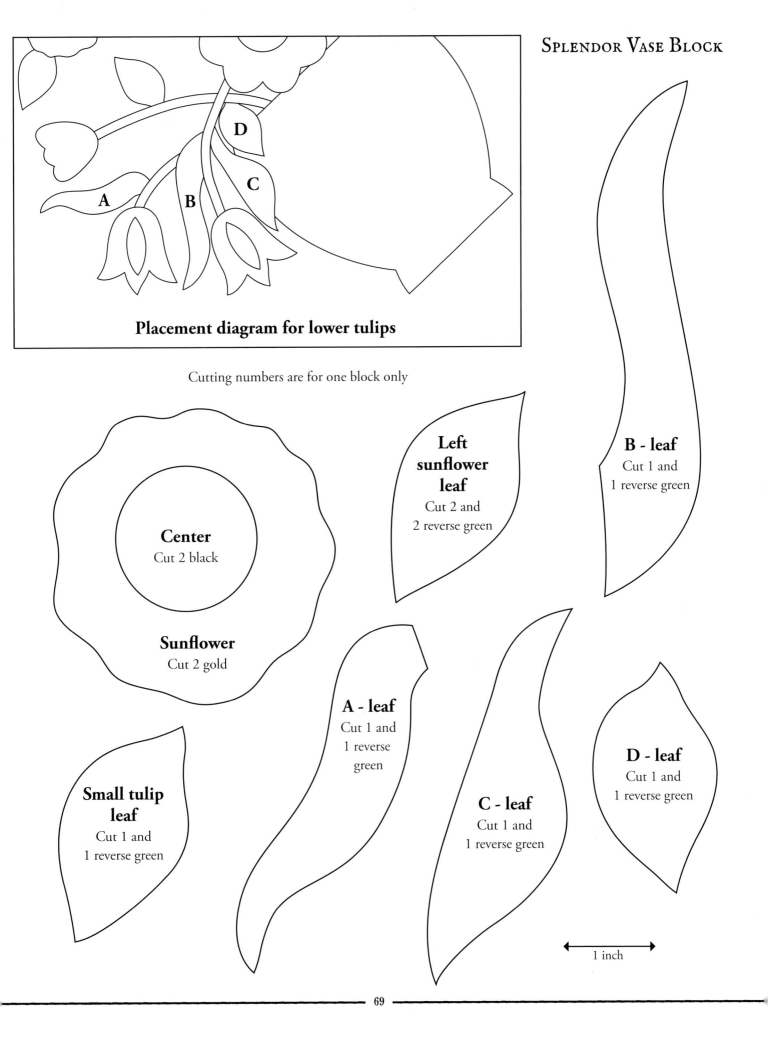

Placement diagram for lower tulips

Cutting numbers are for one block only

Center
Cut 2 black

Sunflower
Cut 2 gold

Left sunflower leaf
Cut 2 and 2 reverse green

B - leaf
Cut 1 and 1 reverse green

A - leaf
Cut 1 and 1 reverse green

Small tulip leaf
Cut 1 and 1 reverse green

C - leaf
Cut 1 and 1 reverse green

D - leaf
Cut 1 and 1 reverse green

1 inch

A B C D

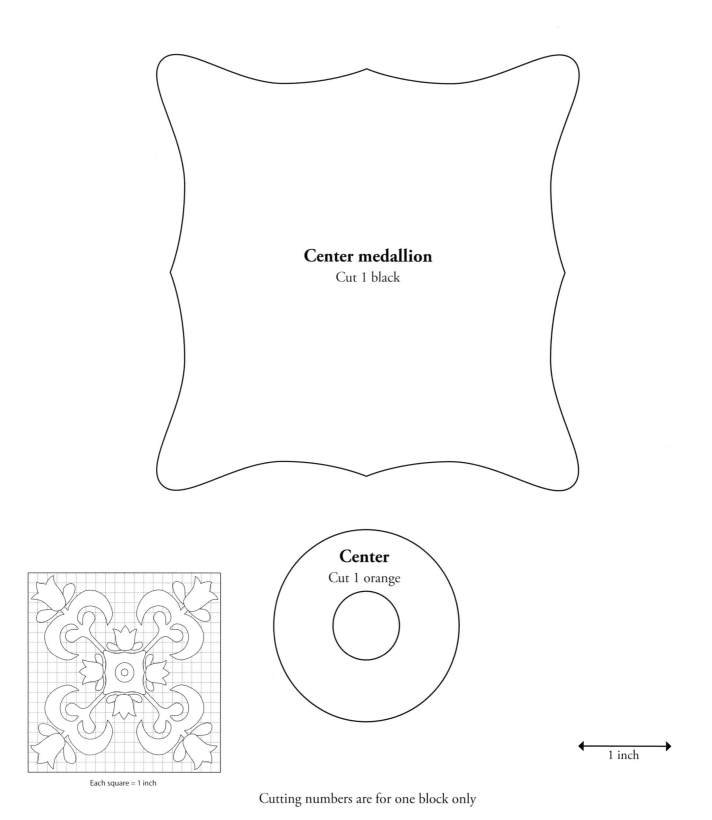

Center medallion
Cut 1 black

Center
Cut 1 orange

Each square = 1 inch

1 inch

Cutting numbers are for one block only

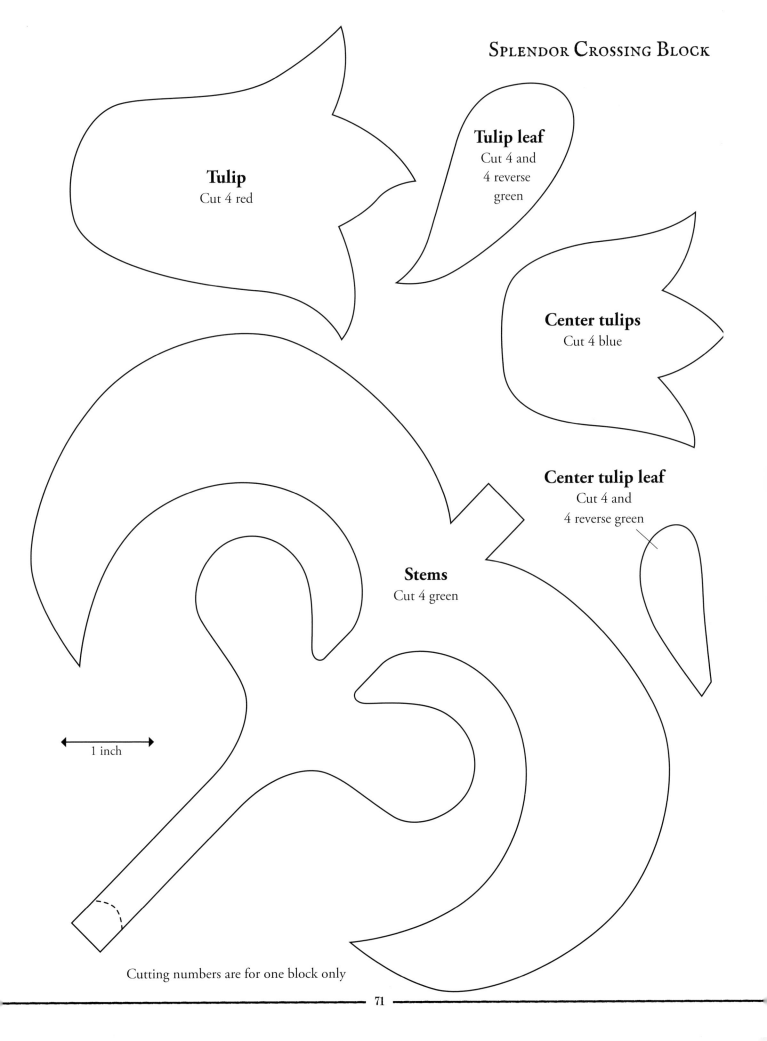

Tulip
Cut 4 red

Tulip leaf
Cut 4 and
4 reverse
green

Center tulips
Cut 4 blue

Center tulip leaf
Cut 4 and
4 reverse green

Stems
Cut 4 green

1 inch

Cutting numbers are for one block only

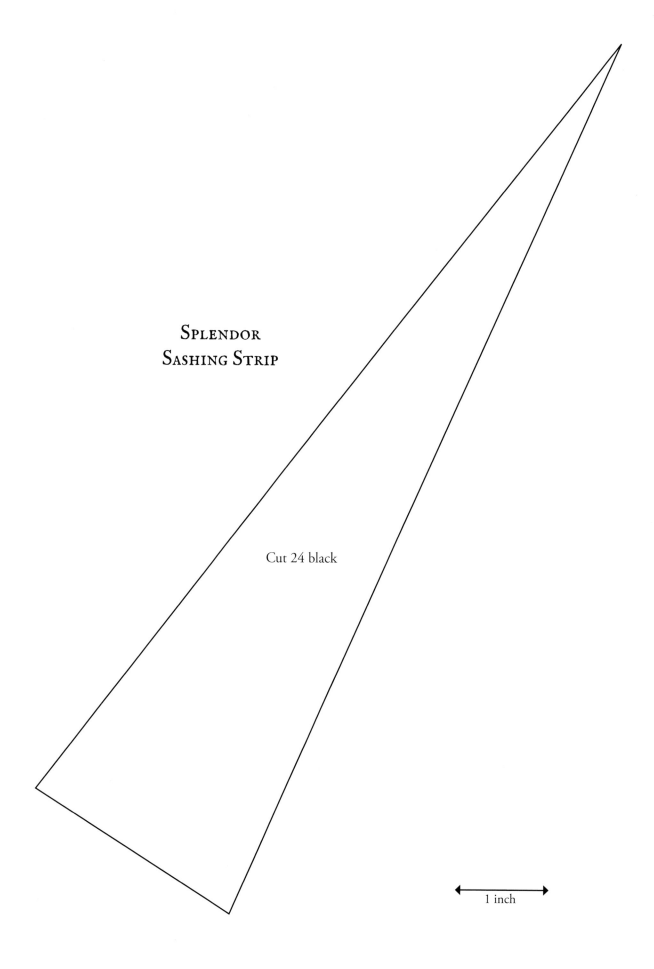

SPLENDOR
SASHING STRIP

Cut 24 black

1 inch

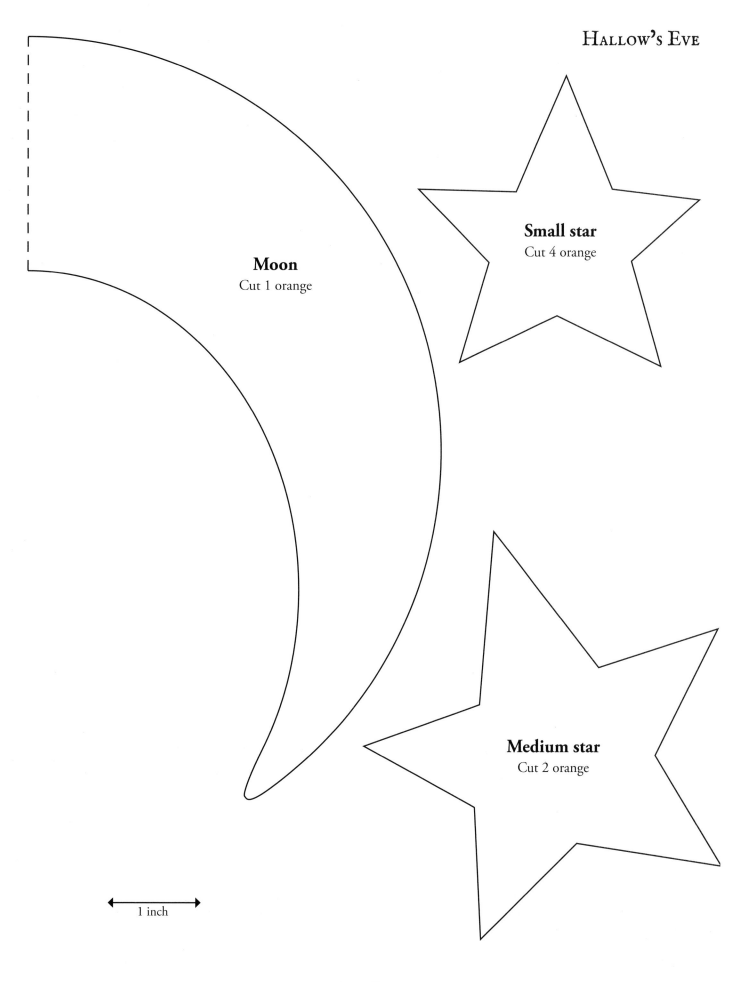

Moon
Cut 1 orange

Small star
Cut 4 orange

Medium star
Cut 2 orange

1 inch

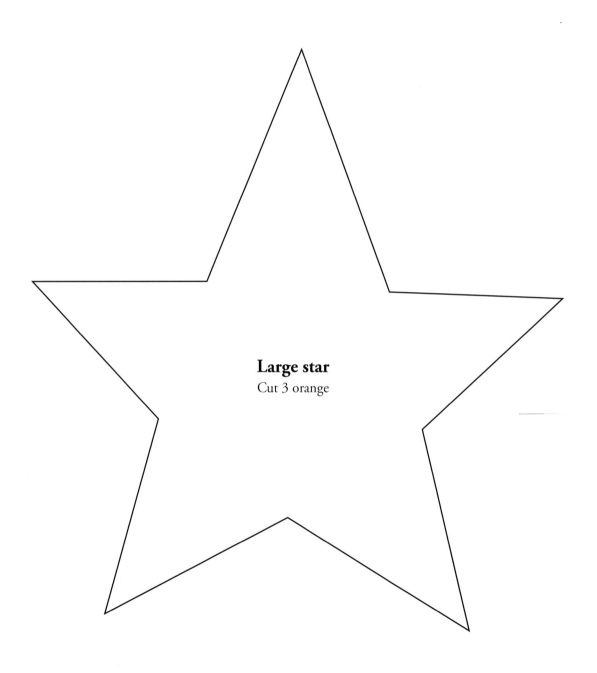

Large star
Cut 3 orange

1 inch

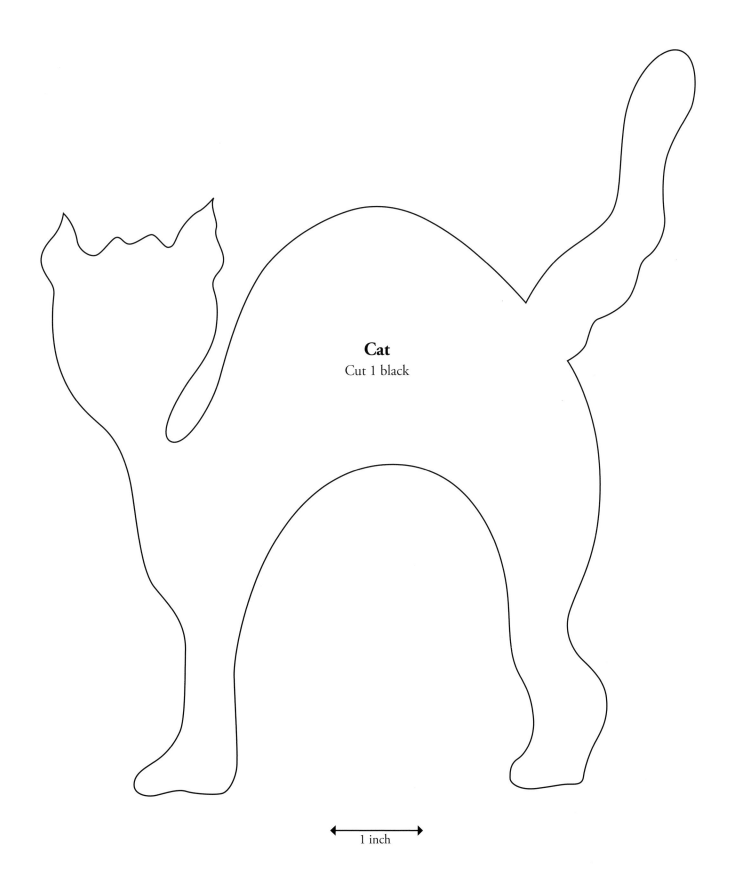

Cat
Cut 1 black

1 inch

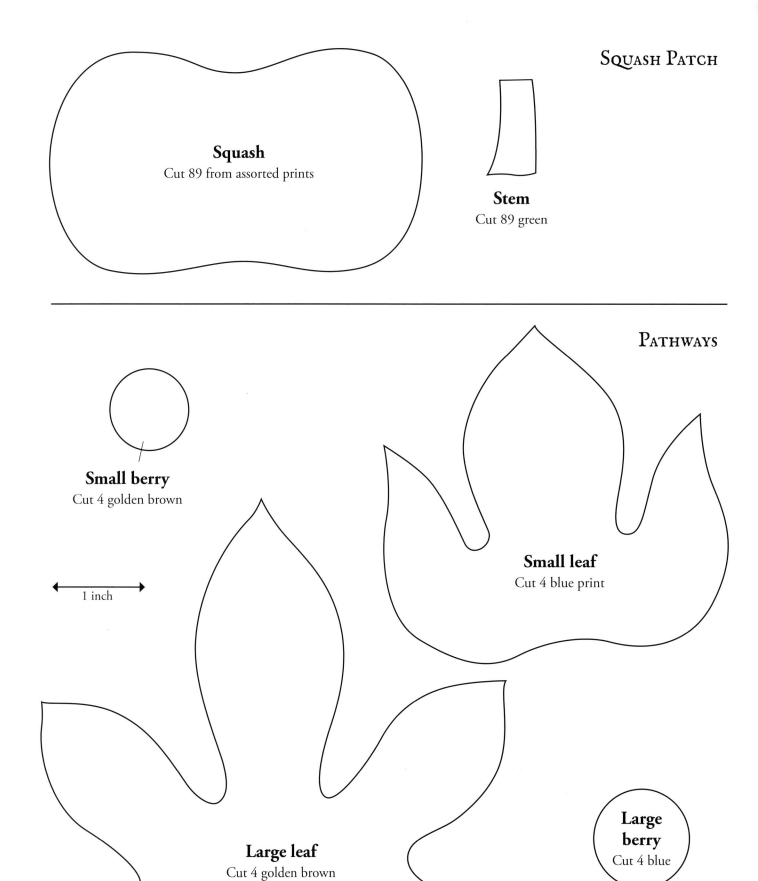

Squash
Cut 89 from assorted prints

Stem
Cut 89 green

Small berry
Cut 4 golden brown

1 inch

Small leaf
Cut 4 blue print

Large leaf
Cut 4 golden brown
and 4 blue print

Large berry
Cut 4 blue

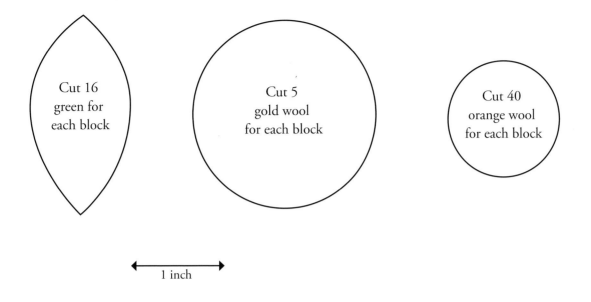

Cut 16
green for
each block

Cut 5
gold wool
for each block

Cut 40
orange wool
for each block

1 inch

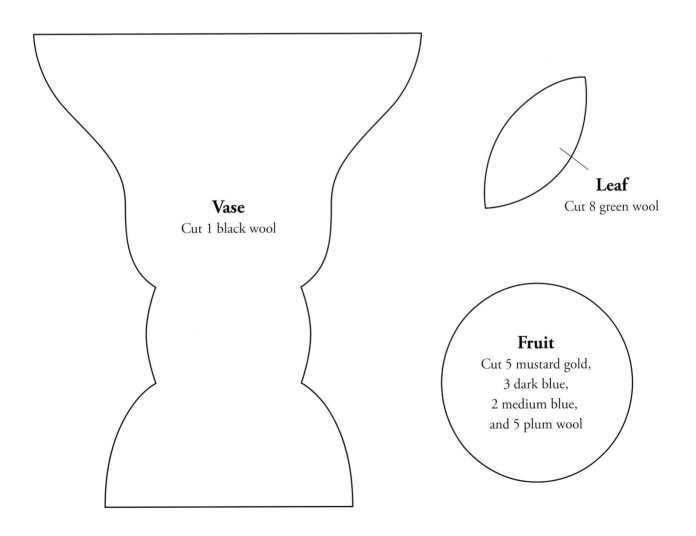

Vase
Cut 1 black wool

Leaf
Cut 8 green wool

Fruit
Cut 5 mustard gold,
3 dark blue,
2 medium blue,
and 5 plum wool

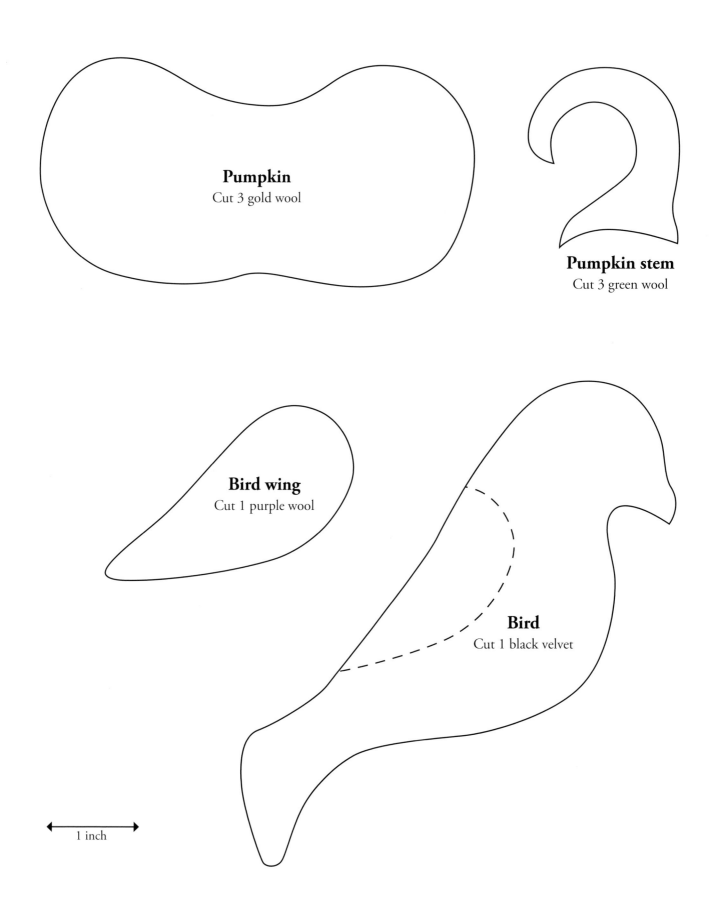

Pumpkin
Cut 3 gold wool

Pumpkin stem
Cut 3 green wool

Bird wing
Cut 1 purple wool

Bird
Cut 1 black velvet

1 inch

NOTES

NOTES